BATS

BY GAIL GIBBONS

HOLIDAY HOUSE / New York

Special thanks to James Doherty
General Curator at the
New York Zoological Society
Bronx, New York

Library of Congress Cataloging-in-Publication Data
Gibbons, Gail.
    Bats/Gail Gibbons. — 1st ed.
    Summary: Describes different kinds of bats, their physical
    characteristics, habits and behavior, and efforts to protect them.
    ISBN 0-8234-1457-4
    1. Bats — Juvenile literature.   [1. Bats.]   I. Title.
    QL737.C5G52   1999
    599.4 — dc21   99-12051
                    CIP
    ISBN 0-8234-1637-2 (pbk.)

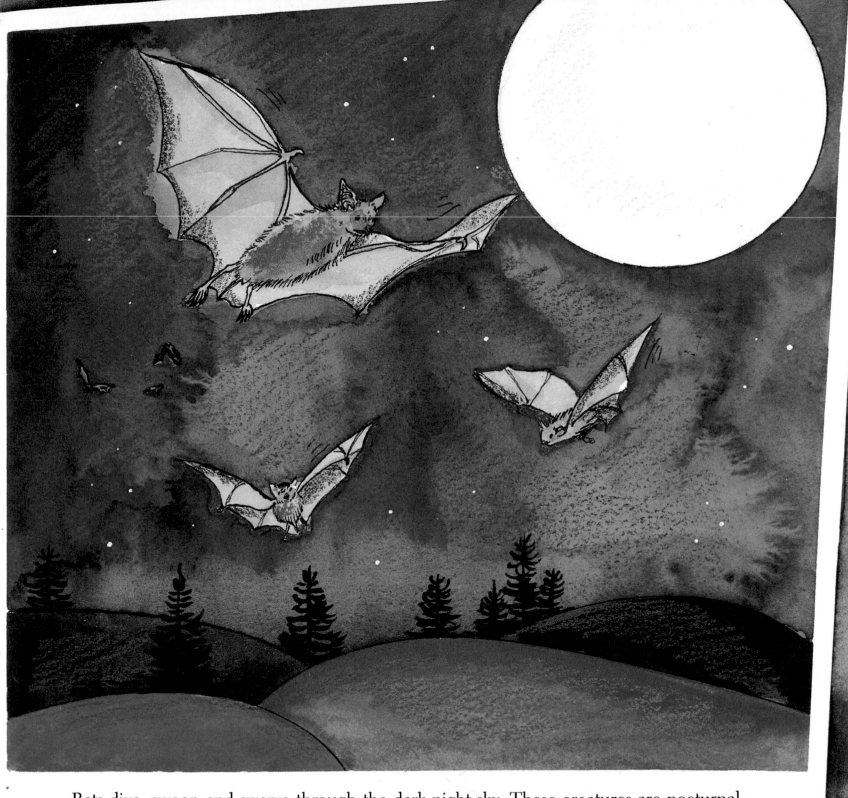

Bats dive, swoop and swerve through the dark night sky. These creatures are nocturnal, meaning they are awake at night and asleep during the day. Most people have never seen a bat.

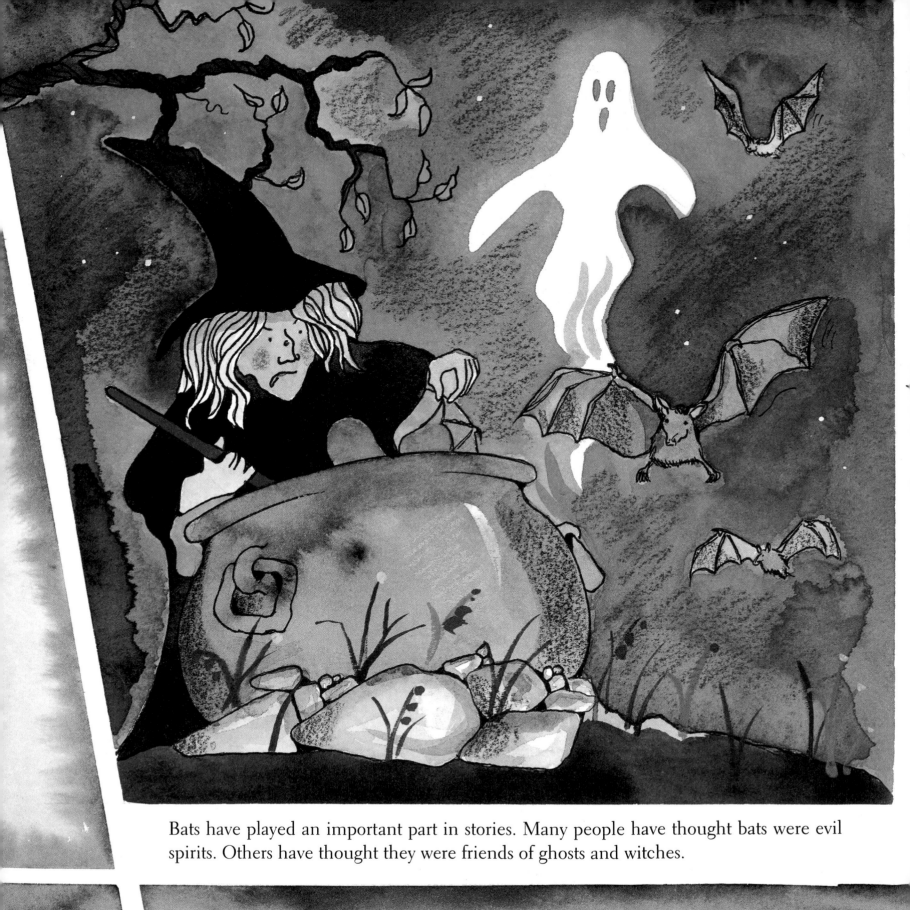

Bats have played an important part in stories. Many people have thought bats were evil spirits. Others have thought they were friends of ghosts and witches.

Because many unkind things have been said about bats, some people still think they are scary. Actually, bats are shy and gentle animals.

FUNNEL-EARED BAT

Bats are mammals, as are dogs, cats and humans. All mammals are warm-blooded animals, and their babies are born alive instead of being hatched from eggs. Bats are the only mammals that can fly.

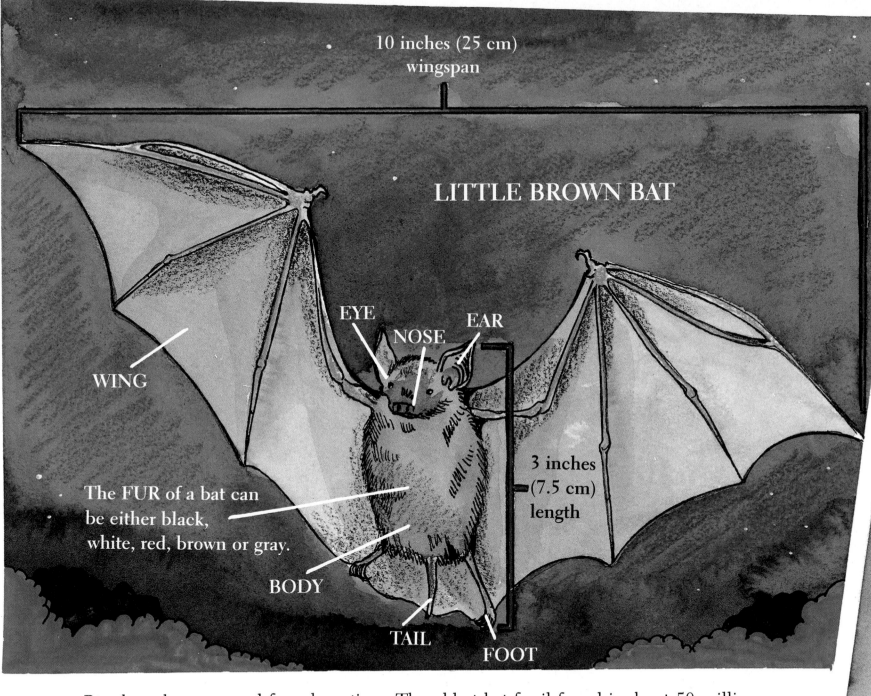

10 inches (25 cm) wingspan

LITTLE BROWN BAT

EYE

NOSE

EAR

WING

The FUR of a bat can be either black, white, red, brown or gray.

3 inches (7.5 cm) length

BODY

TAIL

FOOT

Bats have been around for a long time. The oldest bat fossil found is about 50 million years old. These prehistoric bats looked a lot like today's bats.

All bats have the same basic characteristics, including large wings, small bodies and light-weight bones.

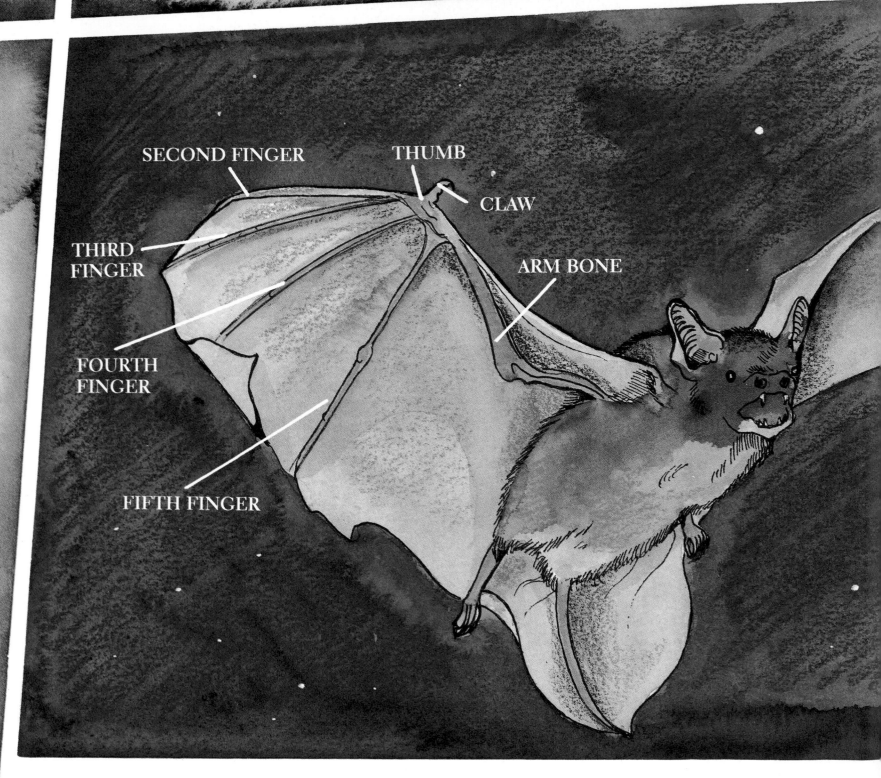

Bat wings are different from the wings of insects or birds. A bat's wing has long arm bones with very long finger bones. A thin skin, called a membrane, stretches between the bones. The thumb ends with a claw.

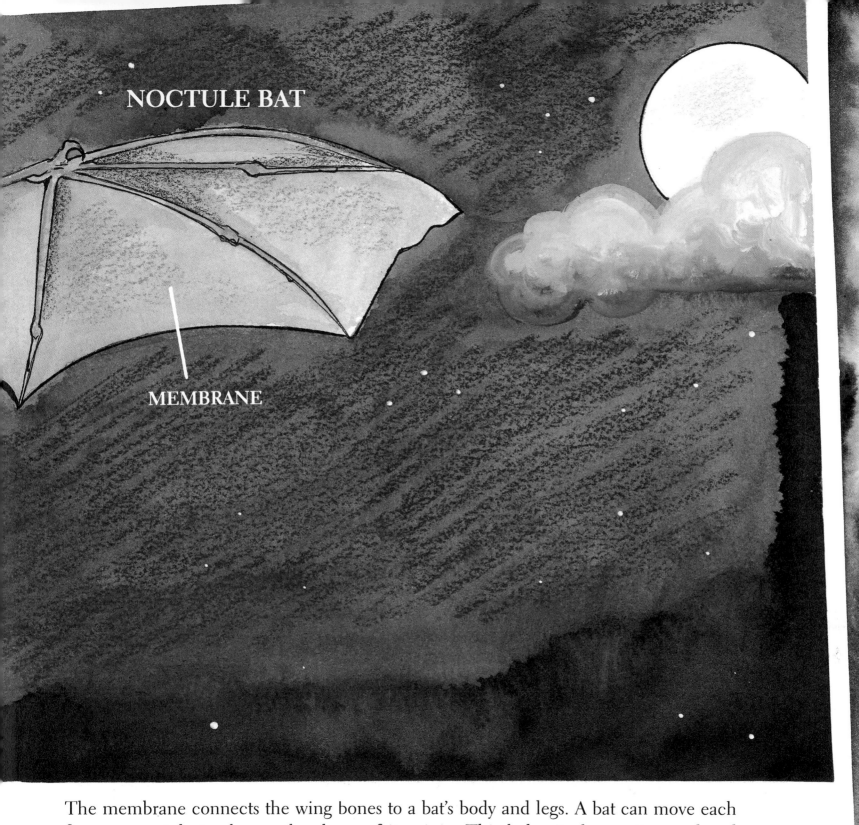

NOCTULE BAT

MEMBRANE

The membrane connects the wing bones to a bat's body and legs. A bat can move each finger separately to change the shape of its wings. This helps it change its speed and direction quickly.

Some bats can fly as fast as 15 miles (24 km) an hour and as high as 10,000 feet (3,050 m).

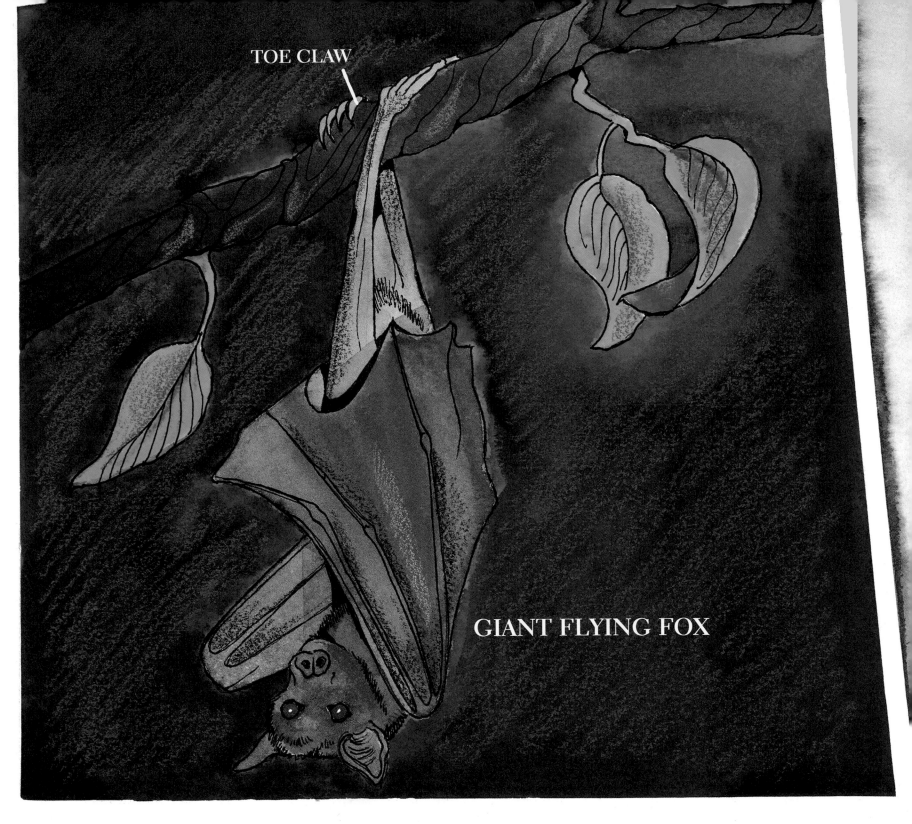

TOE CLAW

GIANT FLYING FOX

When a bat lands, it flips upside down and hangs by its toe claws. It uses these claws to move around.

Bats MIGRATE when they go to and from a warmer climate.

Bats choose many kinds of dark nooks and crannies to live in. These places are called roosts. Many bats live together in caves, attics, barns or tall trees. In places where it gets cold in the winter, some kinds of bats migrate to warmer climates; others use their roosts to hibernate until spring.

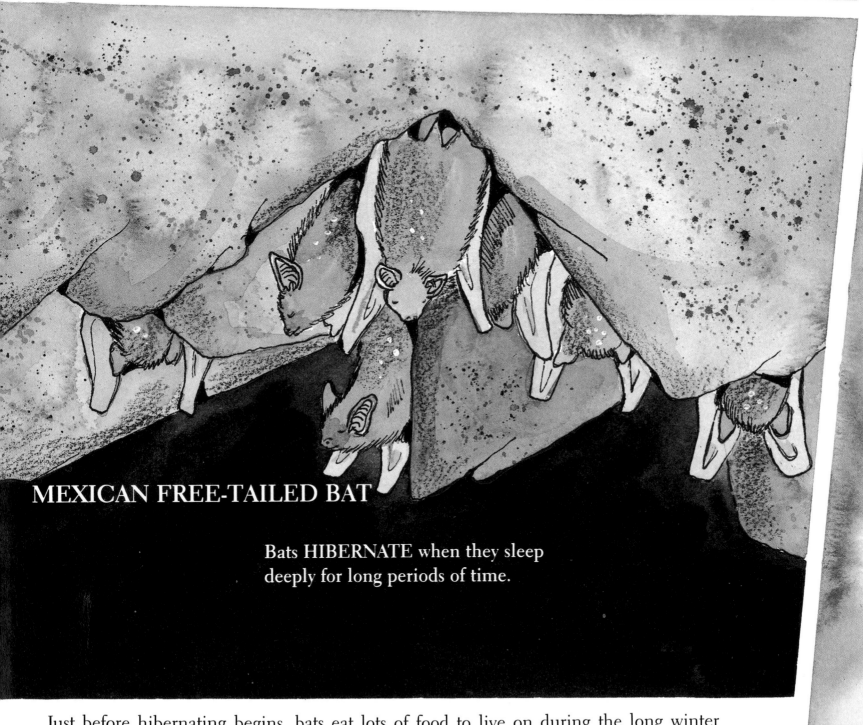

MEXICAN FREE-TAILED BAT

Bats HIBERNATE when they sleep
deeply for long periods of time.

Just before hibernating begins, bats eat lots of food to live on during the long winter months. Their heartbeats slow down, and their body temperatures drop.

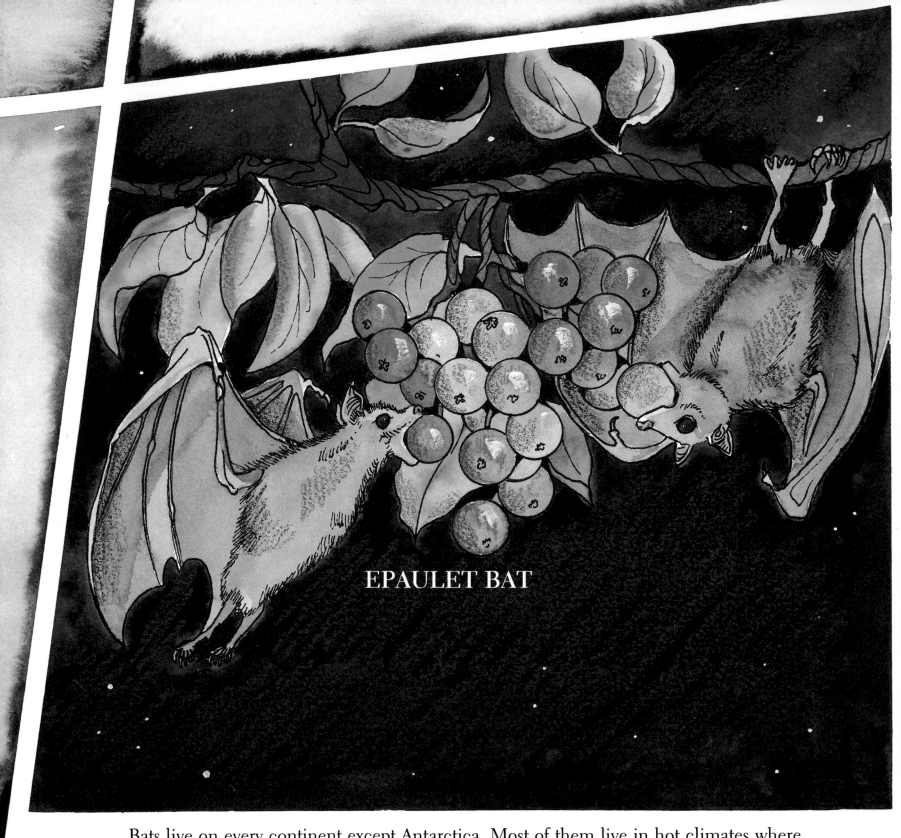

EPAULET BAT

Bats live on every continent except Antarctica. Most of them live in hot climates where there are many insects, fruits and flowers to feed on.

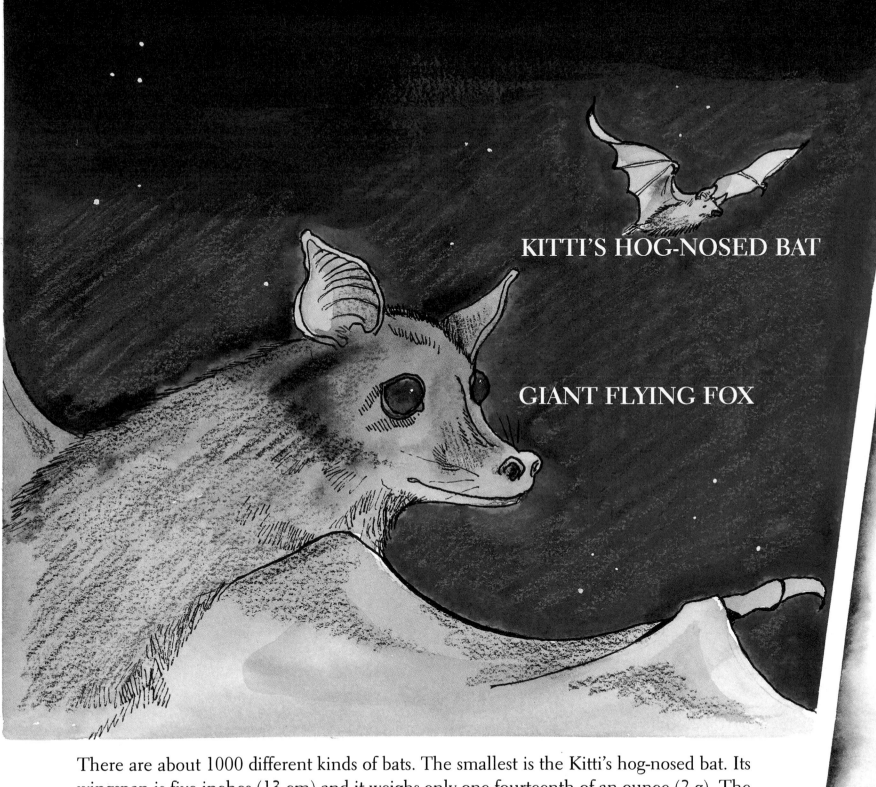

KITTI'S HOG-NOSED BAT

GIANT FLYING FOX

There are about 1000 different kinds of bats. The smallest is the Kitti's hog-nosed bat. Its wingspan is five inches (13 cm) and it weighs only one-fourteenth of an ounce (2 g). The biggest bat is the Giant Flying Fox. It has a wingspan of about five feet (152 cm) and it weighs about two pounds (.9 kg). They both live in Asia.

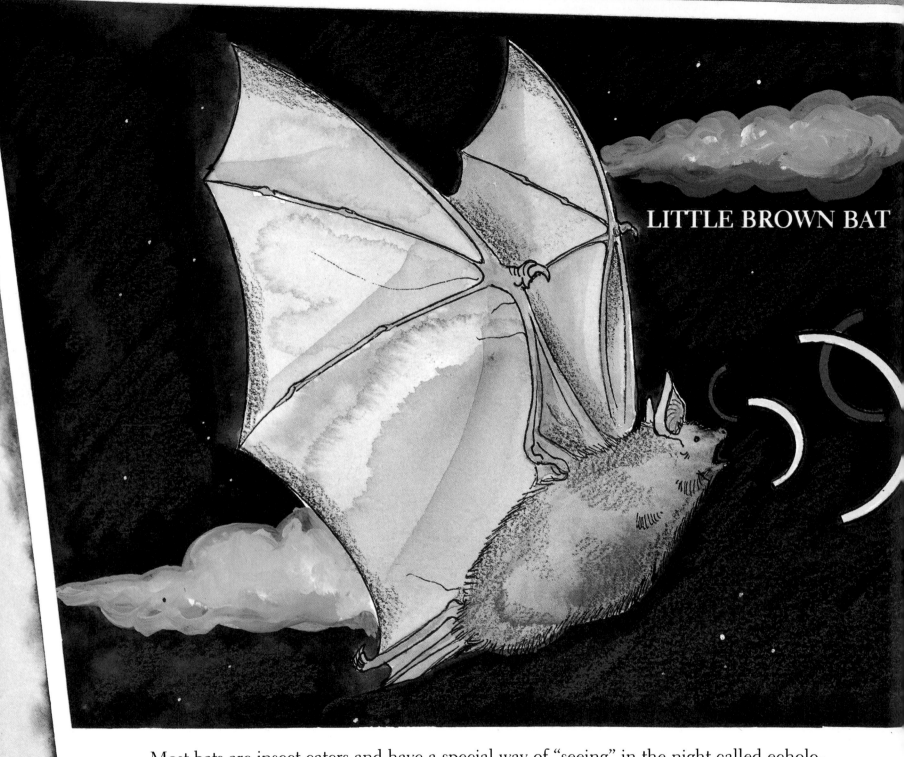

LITTLE BROWN BAT

Most bats are insect eaters and have a special way of "seeing" in the night called echolo-cation. A bat sends out a rapid beeping sound too high-pitched for people to hear.

When hunting, the sound waves hit an insect. The waves bounce back to the bat's ears as echoes. These echoes tell the bat the size and shape of the insect and where it is located. In a flash, the bat scoops up the insect. If it weren't for bats, there would be too many insects.

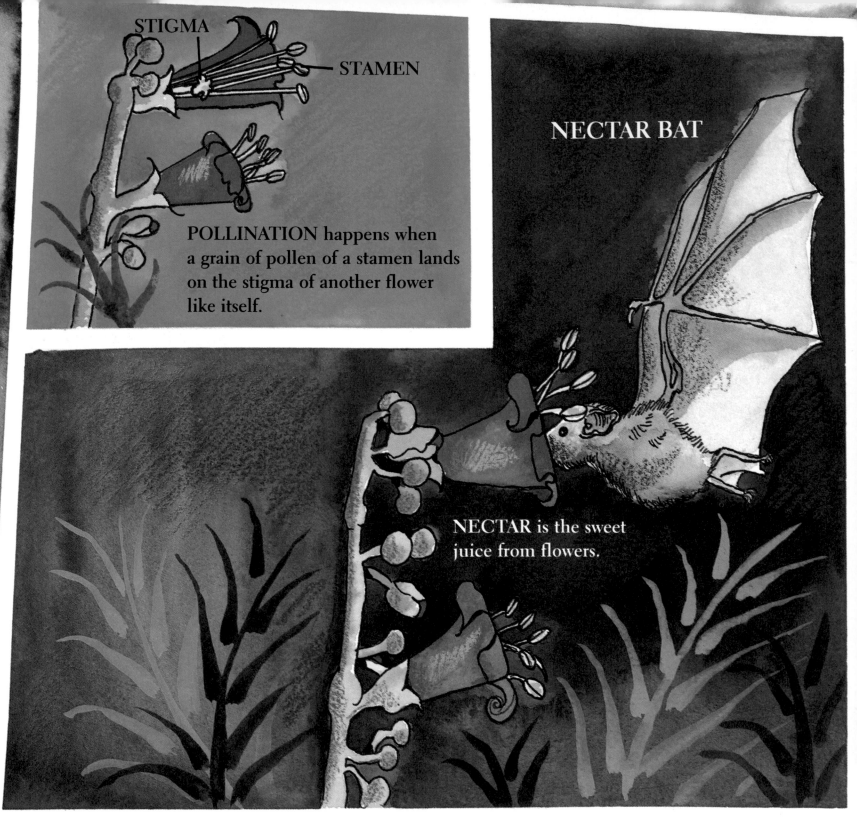

STIGMA

STAMEN

POLLINATION happens when a grain of pollen of a stamen lands on the stigma of another flower like itself.

NECTAR BAT

NECTAR is the sweet juice from flowers.

There are fruit and nectar-eating bats, too. These bats help pollinate plants so we can have foods such as avocados, figs and bananas. They also help scatter seeds.

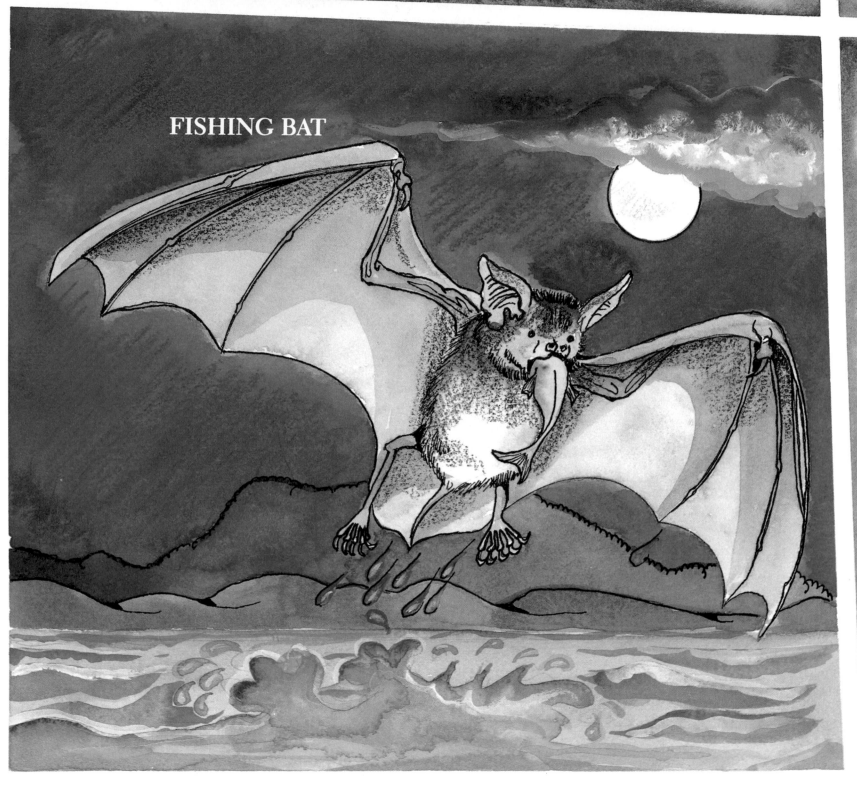

FISHING BAT

A few kinds of bats are meat eaters. They eat fish, frogs, mice and sometimes birds. They have smooth, sharp, crushing teeth that allow them to eat what they catch—bones and all.

VAMPIRE BAT

Blood is the only food for vampire bats. They are found in Mexico, Central America and South America. When the vampire bat finds an animal it makes a tiny cut with its teeth in the animal's skin. Then the bat laps up the blood with its tongue. The animal hardly feels the cut.

Many scary and untrue stories have been told about vampire bats and people called vampires. The famous fictional vampire called Dracula frequently is shown with bats circling him.

DAWN BAT

TUBE-NOSED FRUIT BAT

JAMAICAN FRUIT BAT

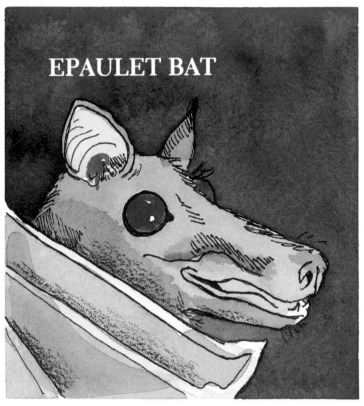

EPAULET BAT

Some bats have long, narrow faces. Others have short, round faces. Some bats have leaf-like shapes on their faces, while others look like dogs.

Most bats have very good hearing and can see well. Most bats have a good sense of smell, too.

In the springtime, female bats gather together in roosts that will become nurseries. There they will give birth to their babies called pups. Most bats have only one pup at a time.

THUMB CLAWS

PUP

LITTLE BROWN BAT

BASKET

During birth the mother bat hangs by her thumb claws with her head up. She forms a basket with her tail membrane. At birth the pup slides from her body into the basket.

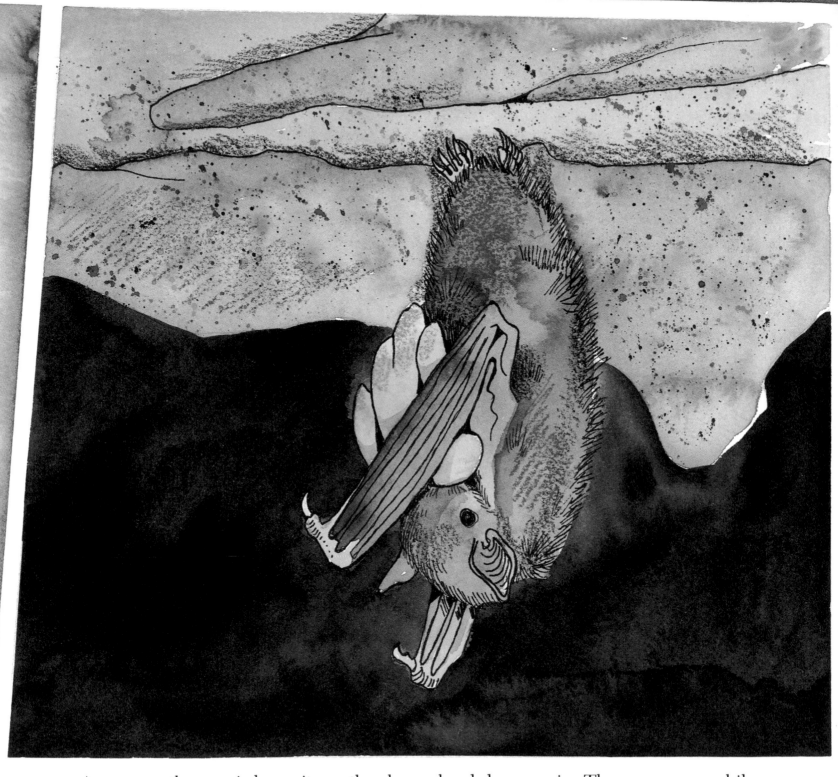

As soon as the pup is born, its mother hangs head down again. The pup nurses while being cradled under the mother's wing. The pup clings to its mother's fur, using its own sharp teeth and claws.

The young pup grows quickly. A ten-day-old pup is almost too heavy for its mother to carry. At three months old, it is flying on nightly hunting trips. When it is about one year old, it is an adult.

Today, in many places bat populations are getting smaller. These bats are endangered. One reason is that many people still don't like bats and destroy their habitats. Other causes are pollution and the use of pesticides for killing crop-damaging insects.

In many places there aren't enough bats left to keep down the number of insect pests or to pollinate flowers.

People are learning how to help protect bats. Some people provide bat houses where they can roost. Sometimes people cover bat cave entrances with grillwork. Bats are free to come and go, but people can't enter. Also, there are nature preserves that protect large groups of bats.

Bats play an important role in nature. It's fun to learn about them.

The Mexican free-tailed bats that live in Bracken Cave near San Antonio, Texas, eat about 250 tons (227,000 kg) of insects a night.

Some bats communicate with each other by using their sense of smell or making sounds.

Almost one half of the bat species living in the United States are endangered.

Have you ever heard the saying "As blind as a bat?" It's not true. Bats can see quite well.

Under the Congress Avenue Bridge in Austin, Texas, one can see more than a million Mexican free-tailed bats roosting. They have become a tourist attraction.

Some people think all bats carry a disease called rabies. This is not true. Bats can get rabies, but no more easily than any other animal.

In China bats are a symbol of good luck.

Never touch a bat you find on the ground. It might try to bite you if it is frightened, and it could be sick.

Most bats live to be 10 to 14 years old.

There are about 40 species of bats found in North America. The most common is the little brown bat. It can eat 600 insects in an hour!